THIS BOOK BELONGS TO:

....

....

WEBSITE:

USERNAME:

PASSWORD:

NOTES:

WEBSITE:

USERNAME:

PASSWORD:

NOTES:

WEBSITE:

USERNAME:

PASSWORD:

NOTES:

WEBSITE:

USERNAME:

PASSWORD:

NOTES:

WEBSITE:
_____

USERNAME:
_____

PASSWORD:
_____

NOTES:
_____

WEBSITE:
_____

USERNAME:
_____

PASSWORD:
_____

NOTES:
_____

WEBSITE:
_____

USERNAME:
_____

PASSWORD:
_____

NOTES:
_____

WEBSITE:
_____

USERNAME:
_____

PASSWORD:
_____

NOTES:
_____

WEBSITE:

USERNAME:

PASSWORD:

NOTES:

WEBSITE:

USERNAME:

PASSWORD:

NOTES:

WEBSITE:

USERNAME:

PASSWORD:

NOTES:

WEBSITE:

USERNAME:

PASSWORD:

NOTES:

WEBSITE:

USERNAME:

PASSWORD:

NOTES:

WEBSITE:

USERNAME:

PASSWORD:

NOTES:

WEBSITE:

USERNAME:

PASSWORD:

NOTES:

WEBSITE:

USERNAME:

PASSWORD:

NOTES:

WEBSITE:

USERNAME:

PASSWORD:

NOTES:

WEBSITE:

USERNAME:

PASSWORD:

NOTES:

WEBSITE:

USERNAME:

PASSWORD:

NOTES:

WEBSITE:

USERNAME:

PASSWORD:

NOTES:

WEBSITE:
_____

USERNAME:
_____

PASSWORD:
_____

NOTES:
_____

WEBSITE:
_____

USERNAME:
_____

PASSWORD:
_____

NOTES:
_____

WEBSITE:
_____

USERNAME:
_____

PASSWORD:
_____

NOTES:
_____

WEBSITE:
_____

USERNAME:
_____

PASSWORD:
_____

NOTES:
_____

WEBSITE:

USERNAME:

PASSWORD:

NOTES:

WEBSITE:

USERNAME:

PASSWORD:

NOTES:

WEBSITE:

USERNAME:

PASSWORD:

NOTES:

WEBSITE:

USERNAME:

PASSWORD:

NOTES:

WEBSITE:

USERNAME:

PASSWORD:

NOTES:

WEBSITE:

USERNAME:

PASSWORD:

NOTES:

WEBSITE:

USERNAME:

PASSWORD:

NOTES:

WEBSITE:

USERNAME:

PASSWORD:

NOTES:

WEBSITE:

USERNAME:

PASSWORD:

NOTES:

WEBSITE:

USERNAME:

PASSWORD:

NOTES:

WEBSITE:

USERNAME:

PASSWORD:

NOTES:

WEBSITE:

USERNAME:

PASSWORD:

NOTES:

WEBSITE:

USERNAME:

PASSWORD:

NOTES:

WEBSITE:

USERNAME:

PASSWORD:

NOTES:

WEBSITE:

USERNAME:

PASSWORD:

NOTES:

WEBSITE:

USERNAME:

PASSWORD:

NOTES:

WEBSITE:

USERNAME:

PASSWORD:

NOTES:

WEBSITE:

USERNAME:

PASSWORD:

NOTES:

WEBSITE:

USERNAME:

PASSWORD:

NOTES:

WEBSITE:

USERNAME:

PASSWORD:

NOTES:

WEBSITE:

USERNAME:

PASSWORD:

NOTES:

WEBSITE:

USERNAME:

PASSWORD:

NOTES:

WEBSITE:

USERNAME:

PASSWORD:

NOTES:

WEBSITE:

USERNAME:

PASSWORD:

NOTES:

WEBSITE:

USERNAME:

PASSWORD:

NOTES:

WEBSITE:

USERNAME:

PASSWORD:

NOTES:

WEBSITE:

USERNAME:

PASSWORD:

NOTES:

WEBSITE:

USERNAME:

PASSWORD:

NOTES:

WEBSITE:

USERNAME:

PASSWORD:

NOTES:

WEBSITE:

USERNAME:

PASSWORD:

NOTES:

WEBSITE:

USERNAME:

PASSWORD:

NOTES:

WEBSITE:

USERNAME:

PASSWORD:

NOTES:

WEBSITE:

USERNAME:

PASSWORD:

NOTES:

WEBSITE:

USERNAME:

PASSWORD:

NOTES:

WEBSITE:

USERNAME:

PASSWORD:

NOTES:

WEBSITE:

USERNAME:

PASSWORD:

NOTES:

WEBSITE:

USERNAME:

PASSWORD:

NOTES:

WEBSITE:

USERNAME:

PASSWORD:

NOTES:

WEBSITE:

USERNAME:

PASSWORD:

NOTES:

WEBSITE:

USERNAME:

PASSWORD:

NOTES:

WEBSITE:

USERNAME:

PASSWORD:

NOTES:

WEBSITE:

USERNAME:

PASSWORD:

NOTES:

WEBSITE:

USERNAME:

PASSWORD:

NOTES:

WEBSITE:

USERNAME:

PASSWORD:

NOTES:

WEBSITE:

USERNAME:

PASSWORD:

NOTES:

WEBSITE:

USERNAME:

PASSWORD:

NOTES:

WEBSITE:

USERNAME:

PASSWORD:

NOTES:

WEBSITE:

USERNAME:

PASSWORD:

NOTES:

WEBSITE:

USERNAME:

PASSWORD:

NOTES:

WEBSITE:

USERNAME:

PASSWORD:

NOTES:

WEBSITE:

USERNAME:

PASSWORD:

NOTES:

WEBSITE:

USERNAME:

PASSWORD:

NOTES:

WEBSITE:

USERNAME:

PASSWORD:

NOTES:

WEBSITE:

USERNAME:

PASSWORD:

NOTES:

WEBSITE:

USERNAME:

PASSWORD:

NOTES:

WEBSITE:

USERNAME:

PASSWORD:

NOTES:

WEBSITE:

USERNAME:

PASSWORD:

NOTES:

WEBSITE:

USERNAME:

PASSWORD:

NOTES:

WEBSITE:

USERNAME:

PASSWORD:

NOTES:

WEBSITE:

USERNAME:

PASSWORD:

NOTES:

WEBSITE:

USERNAME:

PASSWORD:

NOTES:

WEBSITE:

USERNAME:

PASSWORD:

NOTES:

WEBSITE:

USERNAME:

PASSWORD:

NOTES:

WEBSITE:

USERNAME:

PASSWORD:

NOTES:

WEBSITE:

USERNAME:

PASSWORD:

NOTES:

WEBSITE:

USERNAME:

PASSWORD:

NOTES:

WEBSITE:

USERNAME:

PASSWORD:

NOTES:

WEBSITE:

USERNAME:

PASSWORD:

NOTES:

WEBSITE:

USERNAME:

PASSWORD:

NOTES:

WEBSITE:

USERNAME:

PASSWORD:

NOTES:

WEBSITE:

USERNAME:

PASSWORD:

NOTES:

WEBSITE:

USERNAME:

PASSWORD:

NOTES:

WEBSITE:

USERNAME:

PASSWORD:

NOTES:

WEBSITE:

USERNAME:

PASSWORD:

NOTES:

WEBSITE:

USERNAME:

PASSWORD:

NOTES:

WEBSITE:

USERNAME:

PASSWORD:

NOTES:

WEBSITE:

USERNAME:

PASSWORD:

NOTES:

WEBSITE:

USERNAME:

PASSWORD:

NOTES:

WEBSITE:

USERNAME:

PASSWORD:

NOTES:

WEBSITE:

USERNAME:

PASSWORD:

NOTES:

WEBSITE:

USERNAME:

PASSWORD:

NOTES:

WEBSITE:

USERNAME:

PASSWORD:

NOTES:

WEBSITE:

USERNAME:

PASSWORD:

NOTES:

WEBSITE:

USERNAME:

PASSWORD:

NOTES:

WEBSITE:

USERNAME:

PASSWORD:

NOTES:

WEBSITE:

USERNAME:

PASSWORD:

NOTES:

WEBSITE:

USERNAME:

PASSWORD:

NOTES:

WEBSITE:

USERNAME:

PASSWORD:

NOTES:

WEBSITE:

USERNAME:

PASSWORD:

NOTES:

WEBSITE:

USERNAME:

PASSWORD:

NOTES:

WEBSITE:

USERNAME:

PASSWORD:

NOTES:

WEBSITE:

USERNAME:

PASSWORD:

NOTES:

WEBSITE:

USERNAME:

PASSWORD:

NOTES:

WEBSITE:

USERNAME:

PASSWORD:

NOTES:

WEBSITE:

USERNAME:

PASSWORD:

NOTES:

WEBSITE:

USERNAME:

PASSWORD:

NOTES:

WEBSITE:

USERNAME:

PASSWORD:

NOTES:

WEBSITE:

USERNAME:

PASSWORD:

NOTES:

WEBSITE:

USERNAME:

PASSWORD:

NOTES:

WEBSITE:

USERNAME:

PASSWORD:

NOTES:

WEBSITE:

USERNAME:

PASSWORD:

NOTES:

WEBSITE:

USERNAME:

PASSWORD:

NOTES:

WEBSITE:

USERNAME:

PASSWORD:

NOTES:

WEBSITE:

USERNAME:

PASSWORD:

NOTES:

WEBSITE:

USERNAME:

PASSWORD:

NOTES:

WEBSITE:

USERNAME:

PASSWORD:

NOTES:

WEBSITE:

USERNAME:

PASSWORD:

NOTES:

WEBSITE:

USERNAME:

PASSWORD:

NOTES:

WEBSITE:

USERNAME:

PASSWORD:

NOTES:

WEBSITE:

USERNAME:

PASSWORD:

NOTES:

WEBSITE:

USERNAME:

PASSWORD:

NOTES:

WEBSITE:

USERNAME:

PASSWORD:

NOTES:

WEBSITE:

USERNAME:

PASSWORD:

NOTES:

WEBSITE:

USERNAME:

PASSWORD:

NOTES:

WEBSITE:

USERNAME:

PASSWORD:

NOTES:

WEBSITE:

USERNAME:

PASSWORD:

NOTES:

WEBSITE:

USERNAME:

PASSWORD:

NOTES:

WEBSITE:

USERNAME:

PASSWORD:

NOTES:

WEBSITE:

USERNAME:

PASSWORD:

NOTES:

WEBSITE:

USERNAME:

PASSWORD:

NOTES:

WEBSITE:

USERNAME:

PASSWORD:

NOTES:

WEBSITE:

USERNAME:

PASSWORD:

NOTES:

WEBSITE:

USERNAME:

PASSWORD:

NOTES:

WEBSITE:

USERNAME:

PASSWORD:

NOTES:

WEBSITE:

USERNAME:

PASSWORD:

NOTES:

WEBSITE:

USERNAME:

PASSWORD:

NOTES:

WEBSITE:

USERNAME:

PASSWORD:

NOTES:

WEBSITE:

USERNAME:

PASSWORD:

NOTES:

WEBSITE:

USERNAME:

PASSWORD:

NOTES:

WEBSITE:

USERNAME:

PASSWORD:

NOTES:

WEBSITE:

USERNAME:

PASSWORD:

NOTES:

WEBSITE:

USERNAME:

PASSWORD:

NOTES:

WEBSITE:

USERNAME:

PASSWORD:

NOTES:

WEBSITE:

USERNAME:

PASSWORD:

NOTES:

WEBSITE:

USERNAME:

PASSWORD:

NOTES:

WEBSITE:

USERNAME:

PASSWORD:

NOTES:

WEBSITE:

USERNAME:

PASSWORD:

NOTES:

WEBSITE:

USERNAME:

PASSWORD:

NOTES:

WEBSITE:

USERNAME:

PASSWORD:

NOTES:

WEBSITE:

USERNAME:

PASSWORD:

NOTES:

WEBSITE:

USERNAME:

PASSWORD:

NOTES:

WEBSITE:

USERNAME:

PASSWORD:

NOTES:

WEBSITE:

USERNAME:

PASSWORD:

NOTES:

WEBSITE:

USERNAME:

PASSWORD:

NOTES:

WEBSITE:

USERNAME:

PASSWORD:

NOTES:

WEBSITE:

USERNAME:

PASSWORD:

NOTES:

WEBSITE:

USERNAME:

PASSWORD:

NOTES:

WEBSITE:

USERNAME:

PASSWORD:

NOTES:

WEBSITE:

USERNAME:

PASSWORD:

NOTES:

WEBSITE:

USERNAME:

PASSWORD:

NOTES:

WEBSITE:

USERNAME:

PASSWORD:

NOTES:

WEBSITE:

USERNAME:

PASSWORD:

NOTES:

WEBSITE:

USERNAME:

PASSWORD:

NOTES:

WEBSITE:

USERNAME:

PASSWORD:

NOTES:

WEBSITE:

USERNAME:

PASSWORD:

NOTES:

WEBSITE:

USERNAME:

PASSWORD:

NOTES:

WEBSITE:

USERNAME:

PASSWORD:

NOTES:

WEBSITE:

USERNAME:

PASSWORD:

NOTES:

WEBSITE:

USERNAME:

PASSWORD:

NOTES:

WEBSITE:

USERNAME:

PASSWORD:

NOTES:

WEBSITE:

USERNAME:

PASSWORD:

NOTES:

WEBSITE:

USERNAME:

PASSWORD:

NOTES:

WEBSITE:

USERNAME:

PASSWORD:

NOTES:

WEBSITE:

USERNAME:

PASSWORD:

NOTES:

WEBSITE:

USERNAME:

PASSWORD:

NOTES:

WEBSITE:

USERNAME:

PASSWORD:

NOTES:

WEBSITE:

USERNAME:

PASSWORD:

NOTES:

WEBSITE:

USERNAME:

PASSWORD:

NOTES:

WEBSITE:

USERNAME:

PASSWORD:

NOTES:

WEBSITE:

USERNAME:

PASSWORD:

NOTES:

WEBSITE:

USERNAME:

PASSWORD:

NOTES:

WEBSITE:

USERNAME:

PASSWORD:

NOTES:

WEBSITE:

USERNAME:

PASSWORD:

NOTES:

WEBSITE:

USERNAME:

PASSWORD:

NOTES:

WEBSITE:

USERNAME:

PASSWORD:

NOTES:

WEBSITE:

USERNAME:

PASSWORD:

NOTES:

Z

WEBSITE:

USERNAME:

PASSWORD:

NOTES:

WEBSITE:

USERNAME:

PASSWORD:

NOTES:

WEBSITE:

USERNAME:

PASSWORD:

NOTES:

WEBSITE:

USERNAME:

PASSWORD:

NOTES:

WEBSITE:

USERNAME:

PASSWORD:

NOTES:

WEBSITE:

USERNAME:

PASSWORD:

NOTES:

WEBSITE:

USERNAME:

PASSWORD:

NOTES:

WEBSITE:

USERNAME:

PASSWORD:

NOTES:

PHONE NUMBERS

....

....

....

....

....

....

....

....

....

....

....

....

....

....

PHONE NUMBERS

....

....

....

....

....

....

....

....

....

....

....

....

....

....

PHONE NUMBERS

....

....

....

....

....

....

....

....

....

....

....

....

....

....

....

PHONE NUMBERS

....

....

....

....

....

....

....

....

....

....

....

....

....

....

PHONE NUMBERS

....

....

....

....

....

....

....

....

....

....

....

....

....

....

PHONE NUMBERS

....

....

....

....

....

....

....

....

....

....

....

....

....

....

PHONE NUMBERS

....

....

....

....

....

....

....

....

....

....

....

....

....

....

....

PHONE NUMBERS

....

....

....

....

....

....

....

....

....

....

....

....

....

....

PHONE NUMBERS

....

....

....

....

....

....

....

....

....

....

....

....

....

....

PHONE NUMBERS

....

....

....

....

....

....

....

....

....

....

....

....

....

....

....

ADDRESSES

....

....

....

....

....

....

....

....

....

....

....

....

....

....

....

ADDRESSES

....

....

....

....

....

....

....

....

....

....

....

....

....

....

ADDRESSES

....

....

....

....

....

....

....

....

....

....

....

....

....

....

ADDRESSES

....

....

....

....

....

....

....

....

....

....

....

....

....

....

ADDRESSES

....
....
....
....
....
....
....
....
....
....
....
....
....
....

ADDRESSES

....

....

....

....

....

....

....

....

....

....

....

....

....

....

ADDRESSES

....

....

....

....

....

....

....

....

....

....

....

....

....

....

ADDRESSES

....

....

....

....

....

....

....

....

....

....

....

....

....

....

ADDRESSES

....
....
....
....
....
....
....
....
....
....
....
....
....
....
....

ADDRESSES

....

....

....

....

....

....

....

....

....

....

....

....

....

....

DATES TO CELEBRATE

JANUARY

....
....
....
....
....
....
....
....
....

FEBRUARY

....
....
....
....
....
....
....
....
....

MARCH

....
....
....
....
....
....
....
....
....

APRIL

....
....
....
....
....
....
....
....

MAY

....
....
....
....
....
....
....
....

JUNE

....
....
....
....
....
....
....
....

DATES TO CELEBRATE

JULY	AUGUST	SEPTEMBER
....	....	....
....	....	....
....	....	....
....	....	....
....	....	....
....	....	....
....	....	....
....	....	....
....	....	....

OCTOBER	NOVEMBER	DECEMBER
....	....	....
....	....	....
....	....	....
....	....	....
....	....	....
....	....	....
....	....	....
....	....	....

NOTES

NOTES

....

....

....

....

....

....

....

....

....

....

....

....

....

....

NOTES

....
....
....
....
....
....
....
....
....
....
....
....
....
....
....

NOTES

....

....

....

....

....

....

....

....

....

....

....

....

....

....

....

NOTES

....
....
....
....
....
....
....
....
....
....
....
....
....
....
....

NOTES

NOTES

....
....
....
....
....
....
....
....
....
....
....
....
....
....
....

NOTES

....

....

....

....

....

....

....

....

....

....

....

....

....

....

NOTES

....

....

....

....

....

....

....

....

....

....

....

....

....

....

....

NOTES

NOTES

··

··

··

··

··

··

··

··

··

··

··

··

··

··

NOTES

....
....
....
....
....
....
....
....
....
....
....
....
....
....
....

NOTES

··
··
··
··
··
··
··
··
··
··
··
··
··
··

NOTES

....

....

....

....

....

....

....

....

....

....

....

....

....

....

NOTES

NOTES

NOTES

NOTES

....

....

....

....

....

....

....

....

....

....

....

....

....

....

NOTES

....

....

....

....

....

....

....

....

....

....

....

....

....

....

....

NOTES

NOTES

....

....

....

....

....

....

....

....

....

....

....

....

....

....

NOTES

···

···

···

···

···

···

···

···

···

···

···

···

···

···

NOTES

....

....

....

....

....

....

....

....

....

....

....

....

....

....

NOTES

....

....

....

....

....

....

....

....

....

....

....

....

....

....

....

NOTES

....

....

....

....

....

....

....

....

....

....

....

....

....

....

NOTES

NOTES

....

....

....

....

....

....

....

....

....

....

....

....

....

....

....

NOTES

....
....
....
....
....
....
....
....
....
....
....
....
....
....
....

NOTES

....

....

....

....

....

....

....

....

....

....

....

....

....

....

NOTES

NOTES

....
....
....
....
....
....
....
....
....
....
....
....
....
....
....

NOTES

....

....

....

....

....

....

....

....

....

....

....

....

....

....

....

NOTES

....
....
....
....
....
....
....
....
....
....
....
....
....
....
....
....

NOTES

NOTES

....

....

....

....

....

....

....

....

....

....

....

....

....

....